Char-Broil Grilling Cookbook for Beginners

365-Day Tasty Succulent Barbecue Recipes for Your Mouthwatering Outdoor Grilling to Amaze Your Family and Friends

Hedy Skolik

Table of Contents

Introduction

Not only is Char-Broil grilling a useful skill to learn, it can also be super fun! This beginner-friendly cookbook is packed with simple recipes to help you level up your grilling skills and create delicious dishes that you'll be proud to share with your friends and family.

With step-by-step guidance, complete with sample meal plans and frequently asked questions, The Char-Broil Grilling Cookbook for Beginners is the only plan you need to experience the incredible benefits of the carnivore diet for yourself.

It is a magic cookbook filled with everything you need to know to enjoy outside grill and join the fun. At its heart is a focus on simplicity rather than complexity, subtraction rather than addition, making this an incredibly effective diet that is also easy to follow.

Chapter 1: Char Broil Smokers

Congratulations on owning a Char-Broil Smoker. Undeniably one of the best smokers on the market. Char-Broil is a widely know manufacturer of premium outdoor stainless outdoor grills. The smoker is everything you could possibly want in a smoker. Whether your beginner or seasoned pro the Char-Broil Smoker Series gives an authentic smokehouse flavor to any dish that you cook. Char-Broil Smokers are the finest on the market today and very user friendly.

Examples of their quality are the heavy-duty plated-steel cooking grates are what I really like. The smokers grill area offers enough space for cooking multiple dishes at the same time. Your actual cooking time is less with more room to cook. You won't be disappointed in the smaller series either. There's plenty of room on the grill too.

The Char-Broil Smokers have lid thermometers for convenience. It easy to check the internal temperatures at just a glance and you don't have to open the lid. The Char-Broil Smoker also features variable damping control for easy venting. With the large Char-Broil Smoker, you can cook a whole turkey and an ham at the same time.

One awesome feature is it's also equipped with a water/wood chip box allowing you to get tender meat that is moist and juicy at just the right low slow cooking temperature every time. Smoked vegetables will be the ultimate cooking experience you won't soon forget.

You'll will enjoy smoking or barbecue grilling with all the Char-Broil Smokers available today. Here are the current models to choose from. It doesn't matter which one you purchase or already own. All the models will give you a great experience smoking meat and vegetables. Now lets smoke!

Char-Broil Smoker Models

- **Digital Electric Smokers**

4 to choose from

- **Vertical Smokers**

Electric Smoker

- **Vertical Propane gas smoker**

Large propane smoker

Charcoal Smoker

- **BBQ Smokers**

BBQ Offset Smoker Grill 430 offset

Deluxe BBQ Offset Smoker Grill 1280

- **The Big Easy Series**

roasting, frying, and smoking all in one.

Smoker Roaster & Grill

Electric 2 in 1 Smoker

Oil less Turkey Fryer

Chapter 2: Char-Broil Wood Types

- **Hickory**

Pungent, smoky, bacon-like flavor.

Pork, chicken, beef, wild game, cheeses.

- **Pecan**

Rich and more subtle than hickory, but similar in taste. Burns cool, so ideal for very low heat smoking.

Pork, chicken, lamb, fish, cheeses.

- **Mesquite**

Sweeter, more delicate flavor than hickory. Tends to burn hot, so use carefully.

Most meats, especially beef. Most vegetables.

- **Alder**

Delicate flavor that enhances lighter meats.

Salmon, swordfish, sturgeon, other fish. Also good with chicken and pork.

- **Oak**

Forthright but pleasant flavor. Blends well with a variety of textures and flavors.

Beef (particularly brisket), poultry, pork.

- **Maple**

Mildly smoky, somewhat sweet flavor. Try mixing maple with corncobs for ham or bacon.

Poultry, vegetables, ham.

- **Cherry**

Slightly sweet, fruity smoke flavor.

Poultry, game birds, pork.

- **Apple**

Slightly sweet but denser, fruity smoke flavor.

Beef, poultry, game birds, pork (particularly ham).

- **Peach or Pear**

Slightly sweet, woodsy flavor.

Poultry, game birds, pork.

- **Grape vines**

Aromatic, similar to fruit woods.

Turkey, chicken, beef.

- **Wine barrel chips**

Wine and oak flavors. A flavorful novelty that smells wonderful, too.

Beef, turkey, chicken, cheeses.

- **Seaweed**

Tangy and smoky flavors. (Wash and dry in sun before use.)

Lobster, crab, shrimp, mussels, clams.

- **Herbs & spices**

(bay leaves, rosemary, garlic, mint, orange or lemon peels, whole nutmeg, cinnamon sticks, and others)

Vary from spicy (bay leaves or garlic) to sweet (other seasonings), delicate to mild. Generally, herbs and spices with higher oil content will provide stronger flavoring.

Soak branches and stems in water before adding to fire. They burn quickly, so you may need to replenish often.

Vegetables, cheeses, and a variety of small pieces of meat (lighter and thin-cut meats, fish steaks and fillets, and kabobs).

Chapter 3: Char-Broil Poultry

Easy Chicken Thighs

Ingredients:

- 6 chicken thighs with the skin on
- 1 cup olive oil
- 2 tbsp paprika
- 2 tbsp chili powder
- 1 tbsp thyme
- 1 tbsp garlic powder
- 2 tbsp cayenne
- 1 tbsp salt
- 2 tbsp black pepper
- Favorite BBQ sauce

Directions:

1. Soak you favorite wood chips in water for 1 hour.
2. Preheat your smoker to a temperature of 250 degrees F.
3. Blend all the dry rub seasoning ingredients thoroughly in a small bowl.
4. Coat olive oil completely on the chicken thighs.
5. Sprinkle the season mix completely over the chicken thighs. Ensure they are fully coated.
6. Arrange your chicken thighs on a smoker rack.
7. Check the thighs every 35 minutes and turnover then baste with barbecue sauce.
8. Total cooking time is 3 to 4 hours total depending on the size of the thighs and the temperature.
9. Check for a final internal temperature of 165 degrees for fully cooked.

Easy Chicken Drumsticks

Ingredients:

- 6 chicken legs
- 1 cup olive oil
- 1 tsp cayenne pepper
- 1 tsp paprika
- 2 tsp salt
- 1 tbsp onion powder
- 1 tsp dried thyme
- 1 tbsp garlic powder
- 1 teaspoon pepper

Directions:

1. Soak the wood in water for 1 hour.
2. Preheat the smoker to 250 degrees.
3. Blend the dry seasoning ingredients together in a small bowl.
4. Rub olive oil all over the chicken legs thoroughly.
5. Rub the dry seasoning on the drum sticks.
6. Arrange the drumsticks on the grill.
7. Smoke for 2 hours and turn them over every 35 minutes.
8. Total cooking time is about 3 to 4 hours.
9. When they reach an internal temperature of 165 degrees the chicken legs are done.
10. Use a sweet fruit wood like apple, pecan, or cherry wood for this recipe.

Tequila Chicken

Ingredients:

- 5 pound whole chicken
- 4 cups Lemon-Lime Tequila Mix
- 1 tbsp garlic powder
- 1 tbsp onion powder
- 1 tbsp salt
- 1 tbsp black pepper

Directions:

1. Put the chicken into a large resealable plastic bag.
2. Mix all seasonings and tequila mix together.
3. Add marinade to bag, seal the bag, and place in the refrigerator overnight.
4. Soak the wood chips in water for 1 hour at least.
5. Preheat smoker to 250 degrees F.
6. Take the chicken from the bag, and place on the rack grate.
7. Lightly sprinkle lemon pepper on the chicken.
8. Cook time is about 4 hours.
9. Make sure the internal temperature of the chicken breast reaches 175 degrees F.
10. Brush the chicken down with olive oil or butter every 45 minutes to keep the chicken moist and give more flavor.

Beer Can Chicken

Ingredients:

- 3 or 4 pound chicken
- 3 Cloves of Garlic
- few pieces of chopped onion
- Beer of your choice

Injection Ingredients:

- 1/2 cup melted butter room temperature
- 2 tablespoons of hot seasoning, more for a spicier chicken.
- tsp garlic powder
- 1 tsp onion powder

Rub Ingredients:

- olive oil
- favorite hot seasoning to cover the outside of the chicken.

Mop Ingredients:

- 1 cup of apple Cider
- 1/2 cup of olive oil a Spray Bottle

Directions:

1. Preheat your smoker to about 250 F degrees.
2. Use hickory for smoking the chicken. Be sure and soak the chips for at least one hour.
3. Mix all injection ingredients together.
4. Using a kitchen syringe, inject the liquid into various spots under the skin of the chicken.
5. Inject about 1/2 of the mixture into the breasts, use the other 1/2 throughout the rest of the chicken.

6. Rub the chicken down with olive oil, and apply an even layer of seasoning on the bird.
7. Put the garlic in the can by widening the hole.
8. Place the bird on the can. It should sit up by itself.
9. Prop the legs forward to make it sit up right.
10. Mix the mop ingredients in the spray bottle and shake before each use.
11. Put the chicken on the smoker and spray the chicken with the mop about every 35 minutes to give it moisture. Cooking time is about 3-4 hours. Check the internal temperature by sticking it in the thickest part of the meat. When it reaches 175 F. degrees the chicken is done.

Rub and Brine Whole Chicken

Ingredients:

- 1 whole chicken
- 1 gallon of water
- 3/4 cup salt
- 1 cup sugar
- 1 tbsp garlic power
- 2 tablespoon of pepper
- 1 tablespoon of cayenne

Rub Recipe Ingredients:

- 1/4 cup olive oil
- 1/4 cup soy sauce
- 2 tbsp onion powder
- 1 tbsp garlic powder
- 2 tbsp cayenne pepper
- 2 tbsp paprika
- 2 tbsp garlic powder or 2 crushed garlic cloves
- 1-1/2 tbsp black pepper
- 1 tsp dried oregano
- 1 tsp dried thyme

Directions:

1. Boil water in a large pot Add the sugar and salt. Let the water cool down.
2. Add the rest of your brine ingredients and the chicken. Soak for 12 hours hrs in the refrigerator.
3. Soak the wood chips in water for 1 hour.
4. Preheat the smoker to 250 degrees F.

5. Blend all of the recipe ingredients together. Coat the chicken inside and out with the rub seasoning fully. Separate the skin from the breast of the chicken by pushing your fingers in between them.
6. Stuff the seasoning on the chicken breast, adds another layer of flavor.
7. Check the chicken about once an hour. Keep temperature at 250 degrees.
8. Cooking time is about 4 hours. Using a thermometer cook until 165 degrees inside.

Buffalo Chicken

Ingredients:

- 1 whole chicken
- 1 cups cayenne pepper seasoning
- 1 tbsp garlic powder
- 1/2 cup of water
- 1/3 cup of chopped onion
- 1 chopped garlic
- 1/3 cup chopped tomato
- 1/2 cup white vinegar
- 1 stick butter
- 1 bottle Louisiana Hot Sauce
- 2 tbsp lemon juice or half the juice of a lemon
- 1 tbsp of honey
- 1/4 cup of red ketchup

Buffalo Rub Ingredients:

- 2-3 tbsp oil vegetable, canola, or olive
- 2 tbsp onion powder
- 2 tbsp cayenne pepper
- 2 tbsp paprika
- 2 tbsp garlic powder or 2 crushed garlic cloves
- 2 tbsp Lawry's seasoning salt
- 1-1/2 tsp black pepper

Directions:

1. Soak your favorite wood chips in water for at least an hour.
2. Preheat the smoker or grill to 250 degrees.
3. Blend your seasoning ingredients together in a bowl.
4. Coat the chicken inside and outside with the buffalo mix.

5. Mix all of the buffalo sauce ingredients together using medium-low heat to melt the stick of butter.
6. Using the mix inject the meat with the buffalo mix.
7. Place on the rack in the smoker. Check every hour and baste.
8. With a meat thermometer stick it in the deepest part of the chicken breast for a temperature of 165 degrees.

Easy Chicken Breasts

Ingredients:

- 5 pound bag of chicken breasts
- 2 teaspoons salt
- 2 teaspoons paprika
- 2 teaspoons garlic powder
- 2 teaspoons garlic salt
- 2 teaspoons black pepper
- 1/2 teaspoon cayenne pepper
- 1 teaspoon dried thyme
- 1 teaspoon dried oregano
- 4 tablespoons brown sugar
- 1 bottle of your favorite barbecue sauce

Directions:

1. Blend the chicken seasonings in a mixing bowl with the barbecue sauce.
2. Arrange the breasts on a rack in your smoker
3. Check the breasts every 35 minute, turnover and baste
4. Cooking time is about 3-4 hours
5. Maintain temperature at 250 degrees.
6. Chicken is done when the internal temperature reaches 160 degrees.

Hickory Chicken

Ingredients:

- 1 large whole chicken 4 lbs
- 2 tsp salt
- 2 tsp black pepper
- 2 tsp paprika
- 2 tsp dried thyme
- 2 tsp garlic salt
- 2 tsp lemon pepper
- 2 tsp cayenne pepper
- 6 tsp olive oil

Directions:

1. Hickory wood chips mixed with apple wood chips.
2. Soak your hickory and apple wood chunks in water for a couple of hours.
3. That allows them to smolder instead of burn out quickly.
4. Preheat the smoker to 250 degrees F.
5. Mix all of the chicken seasonings together in a mixing bowl.
6. Rub all over the chicken.
7. Place the chicken on your smoker and shut the lid.
8. Check your chicken after an hour to make sure it is cooking correctly.
9. Make sure the temperature is holding at about 250 degrees.
10. Total cooking time for a whole chicken will be 3-4 hours.
11. Check the internal temperature of the chicken with a meat thermometer.
12. A temperature of 160 degrees in the middle of the breast means it's done.

Chapter 4: Char-Broil Beef

Spice Baby Spice

Ingredients:

- 1 quart of water
- 1/2 cup of cider vinegar
- 1/4 cup of white sugar
- 1/4 cup of vegetable oil
- 2 tbsp garlic power
- 2 tbsp onion power
- 2 tsp of kosher salt
- 1 tsp of white pepper
- 1/2 lb of chopped jalapeno peppers

Directions:

1. Soak your favorite wood chips for 1 hour.
2. Preheat the smoker to 250 degrees F.
3. Blend all the ingredients in a saucepan and bring to a boil.
4. Simmer for six minutes, then slowly cool to room temperature.
5. Refrigerate the marinade until it's 40 degrees Fahrenheit or less.
6. Brine the ribs in this mixture for twenty four hours.
7. Remove the ribs from the marinade. Don't rinse them.
8. Place on a rack in the smoker.
9. Check the ribs every 30 minutes and baste.
10. I always flip them over and baste them to add as much flavor as possible.
11. Cooking time will be about 6-8 hours for super tender ribs that will tear off the bone easily.
12. Boil the jalapeno marinade for five minutes and strain, set the liquid aside.
13. This will be baste for the ribs.
14. Baste the ribs with this jalapeno marinade mixture every 35 minutes.

15. Remove the finished spare ribs when they tear apart easy with a fork.
16. Let them rest for 15 minutes then slice and serve.

Carlsbad Rib Tips

Ingredients:

- Two tablespoons paprika
- One tablespoon kosher salt
- Two tablespoon onion powder
- Two teaspoons garlic powder
- One-half teaspoon ground black pepper

Directions:

1. Soak the chips in water for 1 hour.
2. Preheat the smoker to 250 degrees F.
3. Blend the ingredients in a bowl and cover the rib tip sections completely.
4. Marinate the rib lets in a beer and hot sauce marinade for a six hours before seasoning.
5. Use the rib tip rub on both sides.
6. Slice the rib tip into two inch sections.
7. Season the pieces generously with the dry rub.
8. Check them every 30 minutes and flip over.
9. Smoke until tender usually 3 to 4 hours or until they tear apart with a fork.

Herbs & Spice Ribs

Ingredients:

- 3 tbsp of onion powder
- 3 tbsp of white sugar
- 2 tbsp of garlic powder
- 2 tbsp of Old Bay seasoning
- 1 tbsp black pepper
- 2 tsp of celery salt
- 2 tsp paprika
- 2 tsp oregano
- 1 tsp kosher or canning salt
- 1/2 tsp cayenne pepper
- 1/2 tsp powdered sage
- 1/2 tsp of ground nutmeg

Directions:

1. Use your favorite wood chips but be sure and soak them for an hour first.
2. Preheat the smoker to 250 degrees F.
3. Mix the ingredients together in a bowl.
4. Spread a light coat on the ribs. Rub it in good.
5. Sprinkle on another heavy coat, shaking off what doesn't stick.
6. Place in the refrigerator overnight. They will have more flavor the longer you let them soak.
7. Turn the ribs over every 35 minutes and baste as you smoke the ribs.
8. Their done when the meat tears easily with a fork.

Texas Hot Ribs

Ingredients:

- one package of your favorite taco seasoning or hot sauce
- one tbsp of onion powder
- one tbsp of garlic powder
- one tsp of black pepper
- one-half tsp cumin
- one-half tsp cayenne pepper to taste

Baste the ribs with a mixture of

- one cup water or beer
- two tbsp vegetable oil
- one tbsp of vinegar
- one tbsp of the rib rub seasoning.

Directions:

1. Soak the wood chips in water for 1 hour. Use your favorite wood, preferably oak or mesquite.
2. Preheat the smoker to 250 degrees F.
3. Blend all of the spices together.
4. Cover the ribs with the mixture, then wrap them in plastic wrap.
5. Refrigerator overnight.
6. Place the ribs on the rack in the smoker.
7. Check every 35 minutes and turn over the baste.
8. Cooking time is about 6 to 8 hours.

Mustard Brisket

Ingredients:

- 1 Brisket
- Spicy mustard

Directions:

1. Soak the wood chips in water for 1 hour.
2. Preheat the smoker to 250 degrees F.
3. Lay the brisket fat side up on the cutting board. Score the fat with a criss cross pattern.
4. Rub in the spicy mustard on the brisket real good.
5. Turn the brisket over and rub the mustard a to the other side as well.
6. Put the brisket on the rack in the smoker.
7. Check every 45 minutes and turnover.
8. Cooking time is 7-8 hours.
9. When the brisket reaches 195°F. it is getting close.
10. Stick a meat thermometer in it to check the temperature.
11. Cool before serving.

Cherry Prime Rib

Ingredients:

- 3-4 lb prime rib
- Olive or vegetable oil
- 2 tbsp garlic powder
- 2 tbsp onion powder
- salt and pepper to your taste
- favorite sauce

Directions:

1. Soak the wood chips in water for an hour. cherry wood for flavor.
2. Preheat the smoker to 250 degrees F.
3. Trim off all the excess fat and lay the meat flat.
4. Coat olive or vegetable oil all over the meat and run it over the sides.
5. Spread your favorite sauce or rub fully.
6. Place the meat on the grill and start smoking.
7. Check the meat every hour to make sure it's cooking evenly.
8. Cooking time is about 6-7 hours.
9. Check with a meat thermometer to be sure the meat is cooked.
10. Internal meat temp should be 140°F.

Char Broil Style Ribs

Ingredients:

- slab of spare ribs
- 1 tbsp paprika
- 1 tbsp kosher salt
- 1 tbsp onion powder
- 1 tbsp garlic powder
- 1/2 tsp ground black pepper

Directions:

1. Blend the ingredients in a small bowl.
2. Coat the rub the slab of ribs completely.
3. Marinate the ribs in a beer and hot sauce marinade for a several hours before seasoning.
4. Place the rack on the smoker.
5. Turn over every 35 minutes.
6. Smoke the ribs until they are tender. Check by tearing them apart with a fork.
7. Smoke the beef ribs at a consistent temperature of 225 degrees F.
8. Cooking time is about 6-8 hours.

Beef Short Ribs

Ingredients:

- 4-5 lbs of beef short rib
- 2 tbsp of kosher salt
- 2 tbsp of black pepper
- 2 tbsp of onion powder
- 3 tbsp of garlic powder,
- 2 tsp of celery salt.

Directions:

1. Soak the wood chips in water for an hour.
2. Preheat the smoker to 250 degrees F.
3. Mix the spices and salt together in a small bowl. Rub the meat on both sides with the mix.
4. Place the short ribs directly into the smoker and check every 35 minutes.
5. Turnover the ribs to make sure their not burning and cooking evenly.
6. Cooking time is about 6-8 hours.
7. They will tear off the bone when they are done. Use two forks to test them.

Chapter 5: Char-Broil Pork

Moms Baby Back Ribs

Marinade Ingredients:

- 2 cups apple juice or cider
- 2 tsp non-iodized salt
- 1 tsp chopped garlic
- 1 tsp chili powder
- 1 tsp white pepper
- 1/2 tsp cayenne pepper

Spice Rub Ingredients:

- 1 tbs onion powder
- 1 tbs granulated sugar
- 1 tsp chili powder
- 1 tsp non-iodized salt
- 1/2 tsp garlic powder
- 1/2 tsp black pepper
- 1/2 tsp cayenne pepper
- 1/2 tsp cumin

Directions:

1. Soak the wood chips n water for 1 hour. Use hickory or oak chips
2. preheat the smoker to 225 degrees F.
3. Mix the ingredients together in a bowl.
4. Marinate the baby back ribs for at least two hours in a large plastic bag or tray.
5. Overnight is better.
6. Rotate the ribs in the marinade once in awhile so both sides get soaked good.
7. Remove the ribs from the marinade and drain them for 4 or 5 minutes.
8. Coat the spice rub on both sides of the ribs.

9. Place the ribs on the rack in the smoker.
10. Turn the ribs over every 45 minutes and baste.
11. Cooking time is about 6-8 hours.
12. Ribs are done when they tear easy with a fork.

Merles Country Ribs

Ingredients:

- 1/4 cup of onion powder
- 2 tablespoons of Kosher salt
- 1 tablespoon of black pepper
- 1 tablespoon of sugar
- 1 teaspoon of mustard powder
- 1 teaspoon of allspice

Directions:

1. Soak your favorite wood chips in water for 1 hour.
2. Preheat the smoker to 225 degrees F.
3. Blend the ingredients together in a bowl.
4. Coat the mixture fully on both sides of the ribs.
5. Cover the ribs and place them in the refrigerator for at least two hours.
6. Overnight is the best if possible.
7. Put on a rack in the smoker and check every 45 minutes.
8. Turn them over and season again.
9. Cooking time is about 5-6 hours.
10. They need to reach 165-180 degrees for tenderness.
11. When they tear apart easily with a fork they are done.

Jim Beam Ribs

Ingredients:

- 1/2 cup of Jim Beam
- 1/2 cup brown sugar
- 1 can of beer
- 2 tbsp soy sauce
- 2 tbsp Worcestershire sauce
- 1 tbsp chopped garlic
- 1 tsp black pepper

Directions:

1. Soak the wood chips in water for 1 hour.
2. Hickory is the wood of choice for this recipe.
3. Preheat the smoker to 230 degrees F.
4. Blend all the ingredients together in a small bowl and set aside.
5. Boil the marinade ingredients in a saucepan.
6. Dissolve the sugar completely. Let to cool.
7. Once cool marinate a whole spare rib slab in the Jim Beam juice overnight.
8. Remove the slab from the marinade and allow it to drain.
9. Pat dry before smoking at 230 degrees Fahrenheit.
10. Put the meat on a rack in the smoker.
11. Now put the marinade in a saucepan and bring to a boil, reducing the liquid to half.
12. Add one cup tomato sauce, one quarter cup cider vinegar, and two tablespoons of molasses then continue to simmer until the liquid thickens stirring slowly.
13. Turn the ribs every 45 minutes and baste with the Jim Beam Marinade.
14. Smoke for 7-8 hours or until they tear easily with a fork.
15. The recipe can also be prepared with beef ribs if you prefer.

Pulled Pork Heaven

Ingredients:

- 2 pork butts 5 lbs each
- 2 pickling salt
- 2 tbs black pepper
- 2 tbs paprika
- 2 tbs garlic powder
- 1 tbs ground cumin
- 1 tbs white sugar
- 1 tbs vinegar barbecue sauce

Directions:

1. Soak your favorite wood chips for 1 hour.
2. Preheat the smoker to 250 degrees F.
3. Mix the spices together in a bowl.
4. Give the butts a good rubbing with some of the vinegar barbecue sauce.
5. Then rub on the seasoning.
6. Set the pork butts aside to soak for at least a couple of hours in the rub.
7. Put the pork butts on a rack in your smoker with the fat side up.
8. After two hours baste it with the vinegar sauce about every hour.
9. Test with a meat thermometer and when the internal temperature reaches 190 degrees remove the pork from the smoker.
10. Wrap or cover it, then let it cool for an hour.
11. This step helps in the final texture and flavor of the pulled pork don't skip it.

Apple Cinnamon Pork Loin

Ingredients:

- 1 pork loin
- 1 tsp onion powder
- 1 tbsp garlic
- 1 tsp paprika
- 1 tsp salt
- 1/2 tsp white pepper
- 1/4 tsp ground cinnamon
- 1/4 tsp fresh grated nutmeg

Directions:

1. Remove all of the membrane and excess fat from the outside.
2. Rub the loin with olive oil, then lightly season it with a bit of the dry rub mixture.
3. Use apple wood chips and soak them for an hour.
4. Place the loin on the grill and cook at 225 degrees Fahrenheit for 4 to 4 hours.
5. Check it every hour and turn it over to make sure it cooks evenly.
6. Cook until the internal temperature reaches 155 degrees with a meat thermometer.
7. Cool before serving
8. Apple Cinnamon Sauce
9. Chop two large or three medium sweet apples finely and put in a medium saucepan.
10. Add 1 tablespoon, sugar, 1/2 teaspoon each of cinnamon, paprika, salt and white pepper, and
11. 2 tablespoons rice wine vinegar.
12. Blend the ingredients together thoroughly.
13. Put the lid on and bring to a boil over medium heat, then lower to a simmer.
14. Simmer until the apples are tender.
15. Slice the loin and top with the sauce.

Louisiana Hot Ribs

Ingredients:

- 1 rack of pork ribs
- 1 cup brown sugar
- 1/2 cup paprika
- 2 1/2 tbsp of ground black pepper
- 2 1/2 tbsp
- 1 tbsp mustard powder
- 1 1/2 tbsp chili powder
- 1 1/2 tbsp garlic powder
- 1 1/2 tbsp onion powder
- 1 tsp cayenne
- 1 can El Pato

Directions:

1. Soak the wood chips in water for 1 hour. Use cherry or apple wood
2. preheat the smoker to 225 degrees F.
3. Blend all the ingredients together in a bowl.
4. Coat the ribs thoroughly with the mixture on all sides.
5. Place on the rack and smoke.
6. Check and turn the ribs over every 35 minutes to cook evenly.
7. Done when they tear apart easily with a fork.
8. Cooking time is about 6 to8 hours.

Char-Broil Bacon

Ingredients:

- 4 lb boneless pork loin
- 1/2 cup dark brown sugar
- 1/2 cup Tender Quick Meat Curing Mix
- 1 tsp coarse ground black pepper

Directions:

1. Soak the wood chips in water for 1 hour.
2. Preheat the smoker to 200 degrees F.
3. Rinse the pork loin with water.
4. Trim off the fat. Rub in the black pepper fully on all sides.
5. Stuff the Tender Quick mix into the loin.
6. Do the same with the brown sugar.
7. Put the loin in a large plastic storage container or food storage bag and refrigerate for 4 days.
8. Rotate it once a day.
9. On the fourth day rinse off and dry the loin off with paper towels.
10. Let the pork air dry while you prepare the smoker.
11. Place the meat on the rack in the smoker.
12. Check every hour.
13. Keep the smoker temperature close to 200 degrees Fahrenheit as much as possible.
14. Remove the pork when it reaches 140 degrees Fahrenheit with a meat thermometer.
15. Cooking time is about 5 to 6 hours.
16. Keep in mind you don't want it to totally cook in the smoker. You just want it to get some smoke flavor.
17. Wrap the bacon in plastic wrap, then in foil, and refrigerate for a minimum of two days before slicing.
18. Cook as you would any regular store bought bacon.

Onion Baby Backs

Ingredients:

- 1 rack of baby back ribs
- 2 packages onion soup mix
- favorite BBQ rib rub
- 4 cups of cold water

Directions:

1. Soak the wood chips in water for 1 hour.
2. Preheat to 250 degrees F.
3. Double the amount of mix.
4. Mix up two package of onion soup mix to four cups of water.
5. Make an aluminum foil boat to hold the ribs and onion soup mix.
6. Place the boat in the smoker and place the meat on it.
7. Smoke the ribs for 6-7 hours turning every 45 minutes and baste.
8. After 2 hours turn the ribs in the foil bone side up.
9. Pour enough liquid to cover the bottom up to 1/2 the height of the ribs.
10. Continue to smoke until tender.
11. They will tear apart easy with a fork when done.

Chapter 6: Char-Broil Seafood

Bacon Oysters

Ingredients:

- 6-7 oysters per person
- bacon thin cut
- garlic powder
- onion powder
- salt and pepper
- toothpicks

Directions:

1. Soak the wood chips in water for 1 hour. Use a sweet fruit wood like cherry, apple
2. Preheat the smoker to 225 degrees F.
3. Pry open and clean the oysters from their shells. Sprinkle on all the seasonings.
4. Wrap each oyster tightly with the bacon strips.
5. Poke the bacon wrapped oysters through with a toothpick to hold everything together.
6. Sprinkle more seasoning on the wrapped oysters and put in the smoker.
7. Smoke for about 1 1/2 to 2 hours or until the bacon starts looking brown and crisp.
8. This will depend on the temperature.

Lake Trout

Ingredients:

- 5 medium trout fillets
- 2 tbsp gherkins finely chopped
- 2 tbsp chives chopped
- 1 tsp garlic powder
- 6 oz crème fraiche
- 1 tbsp horseradish sauce
- juice from 1 lemon
- virgin olive oil
- salt and pepper

Directions:

1. Soak your favorite wood chips in water for 1 hour.
2. Preheat the smoker to 225 degrees F.
3. Mix the chives, crème fraiche, horseradish, lemon juice and gherkins together in a small bowl. Season with salt and pepper to your taste.
4. Coat the fish with the mixture on both sides.
5. Place the trout on the grill and start smoking.
6. Check every 30 minutes and turn over.
7. Fish is done when it flakes apart easy with a fork.
8. Cooking time is about 2-3 hours.

Fish in A Brine

Ingredients:

- 4-5 lbs Fish
- Brine Mix
- 1 gallon water
- 1 ½ cups salt
- ¾ cup brown sugar
- ¼ cup garlic power
- ¼ cup onion powder

Directions:

1. Soak the wood chips in water for 1 hour. Use apple wood
2. Preheat the smoker to 225 degrees F.
3. Mix the brine ingredients together.
4. Cut the fish in half's.
5. Soak the fish in the brine for 12 hours or overnight in the refrigerator.
6. Remove from the refrigerator and place the fish on a rack in the smoker.
7. Check the fish every 45 minutes.
8. Cooking time is about 2-3 hours.
9. Fish is done when it is tender and flakes apart with a fork.

Char-Broil Fish

Ingredients:

- 2 fish fillets 1 lb each use bluefish, mackerel, salmon, haddock
- 1 quart liquid brine

Directions:

1. Soak the fish fillets in a ceramic, glass or stainless-steel bowl with the brine.
2. Cover and refrigerate overnight.
3. Soak the wood chips in water for 1 hour.
4. Preheat the smoker to 200 degrees F.
5. Remove and rinse the fillets quickly to remove surface salt.
6. Dry and let set about 3 hours. Season to your tastes.
7. Place the fillets on a rack in the smoker.
8. You can use a baking or tin foil if the grates are to wide.
9. Check every 30 minutes.
10. Cooking time is about 1-2 hours.

Northern Salmon

Ingredients:

- 5 lbs salmon fillets
- 3 quarts cold water
- 1 quart soy sauce
- 1 1/2 cups brown sugar
- 1 cup pickling salt
- 1 cup granulated sugar
- 1/2 cup honey
- 3 large cloves garlic, crushed
- 1 tbsp
- 1 tbsp Old Bay Seasoning
- 2 tsp white pepper

Directions:

1. Soak the wood chips in water for 1 hour.
2. Preheat the smoker to 225 degrees F.
3. Mix the sugar to one quart of the water.
4. Heat the sugar mixture until the sugar has dissolved, stirring often.
5. Turn off the heat and add the honey stirring until dissolved.
6. Mix in the garlic, onion powder, pepper, old bay and cover the pan.
7. Let it set for 10 minutes.
8. Mix in the spice-syrup mixture, salt, and soy sauce to the remaining two quarts of water.
9. Stir until the salt is dissolved.
10. Refrigerate the brine overnight.
11. Now prepare the salmon. Remove all the pin bones out that are present.
12. Slice the salmon into 2-inch strips.
13. Soak the fish in the brine for six to twelve hours.
14. Fish over one inch thick should brine for eight to twelve hours.

15. Remove the salmon from the brine, rinsing quickly.
16. Place on the rack or a baking sheet.
17. Check every 45 minutes and turn over.
18. Cook until it flakes apart with a fork.

Baja Swordfish

Ingredients:

Swordfish

- One 3-inch-thick chunk swordfish loin, skin removed
- 1 cup kosher salt
- 1 cup sugar
- 2 tbsp black peppercorns
- 2 to 3 tablespoons olive oil

Directions:

1. Mix together 8 cups water with the salt, sugar and pepper in a pot.
2. Bring the mixture to a boil to dissolve the salt and sugar. Set aside to cool completely.
3. Soak the swordfish in the brine in a large plastic bag. Refrigerate for 12 hours or overnight.
4. Take the swordfish out of the brine and rinse under cold water.
5. Pat dry and air dry for at least 1 hour.
6. Coat the fish lightly with olive oil and sprinkle with salt and pepper.
7. Place on the rack and smoke. Check every 35 minutes and turn over.
8. Cooking time is about 2 hours.

White Clam Sauce

- 2 dozen little neck clams
- 2 tbsp olive oil
- 3 cloves garlic, mashed to a paste with a little salt
- 1 small serrano chile, finely diced
- 1 cup white wine
- 1 tbsp cold unsalted butter

- 2 tbsp finely chopped fresh flat-leaf parsley, plus a handful of leaves for garnish
- Zest of 1 lemon
- Salt and freshly ground black pepper

Directions:

1. Remove the meat from half the clams and chop roughly.
2. Heat the olive oil in a medium saucepan over high heat.
3. Add the garlic and chile and cook for a few seconds.
4. Add the wine, bring to a simmer and cook until reduced by half.
5. Add the whole clams, cover the sauce pan and cook, shaking the pan occasionally until the clams open. Usually 5 to 10 minutes.
6. Stir in the butter. Remove from the heat and stir in the chopped parsley and lemon.
7. Taste and season with salt and pepper to taste.
8. Pour the sauce over and around the smoked swordfish, and scatter the parsley leaves on top.

Brine Catfish

Ingredients:

- 3 lbs catfish
- 1 gallon water
- 2 cups salt
- ½ brown sugar
- 3 tsp lemon
- 1 tsp onion powder
- 1 tsp garlic powder
- 1 tsp allspice
- 1 tsp pepper

Directions:

1. Soak the wood chips in water for 1 hour. Use fruit wood such as apple wood orcherry wood
2. Preheat the smoker to 200 degrees F.
3. Mix the brine ingredients in a medium bowl.
4. Soak the fish in the brine for several hours.
5. Rinse the fish off with water and pat dry with a paper towel.
6. Let set for 1 hour.
7. Put a piece of foil on the rack with the fish on it and start smoking.
8. Cook until tender or the fish flakes apart easy with a fork.

West Coast Cedar Plank Salmon

Ingredients:

- 4 or 6 salmon fillets
- 2 cedar planks
- 1 tbsp of lemon juice per salmon fillet
- 1 lemon sliced
- 1 1/2 tbsp of garlic and herb seasoning per salmon fillet
- 1 or 2 bags of wood chips of your choice

Directions:

1. Soak the wood chips and cedar planks in water for 1 hour.
2. Preheat the smoker to 225 degrees F.
3. Mix the garlic and herb seasoning with the lemon juice in a small bowl.
4. Coat both sides of each salmon fillet real thick. Let set.
5. Do this a few hours ahead of time to help all of the seasoning marinate.
6. Place the salmon fillets on the cedar planks and place them in the smoker.
7. Set a slice or two of the lemon on top of each salmon fillet.
8. Check the salmon every 30 minutes and turn over.
9. It should take about 2 to 2 1/2 hours depending on the temperature to fully cook.
10. Salmon is done when it flakes apart with a fork.

Chapter 7: Char-Broil Wild Game

Smoked Bear Roast

Ingredients:

- 5lb Bear Roast
- basil garlic vinegar
- water
- 2 lb potatoes, peeled and sliced
- 1 lb carrots, peeled and sliced
- 2 large onions, quartered
- 10 cloves garlic
- 2 sticks celery thinly sliced
- 1 fresh rosemary
- 1 fresh thyme
- 2 tbsp black pepper
- 2 tbsp black mustard seed crushed
- 4 tbsp Worcestershire sauce
- 3 tbsp nutmeg
- 2 dried Tabasco peppers crushed
- 2 tbsp basil garlic vinegar
- flour optional

Marinade Ingredients:

- 2 tbsp salt
- basil garlic vinegar
- water
- mix the ingredients together with enough liquid to soak the roast in.

Directions:

1. Place the meat in a bag or large dish and marinate the bear roast overnight in the basil-garlic vinegar and water mixture.
2. Put the bear meat on the rack in the smoker.
3. Use the remaining ingredients and pan drippings from the smoker.
4. Mix 2 tablespoons of basil garlic vinegar with it for baste. Baste every 30 minutes and turnover.
5. Check to be sure the internal temperature of the roast at it's thickest point reaches 170-190 degrees.
6. Bear meat should be assumed to carry trichinosis so be sure to cook it all the way through.

Venison

Ingredients:

- 1 quarter cup Worcestershire sauce
- 1 quarter cup Soy Sauce
- 1 can of beer
- 1 quarter cup of maple syrup
- 1 teaspoon black pepper
- 1 half teaspoon onion powder
- 1 half teaspoon garlic powder
- 1 quarter cup of brown sugar
- 1 half teaspoon of powdered cayenne pepper

Directions:

1. Soak the wood chips in water for 1 hour. Use your favorite wood chips.
2. Preheat the smoker to 225 degrees F.
3. Mix the ingredients in a large bow and set aside. Slice the venison into bite sized pieces.
4. Soak the venison in the marinade overnight.
5. Remove the meat from the marinate.
6. Wrap each morsel with sliced bacon.
7. Secure the bacon with a toothpick.
8. Soak the toothpicks in water to keep them from burning.
9. Place the venison on the grill in the smoker.
10. Smoke over high heat for three to five hours or until done.
11. Venison is usually eaten medium rare.

Smoked Venison Jerky

Marinade Ingredients:

- Mix together one half cup each of water and soy sauce.
- one-quarter cup of brown sugar
- one and one-half teaspoons of Cajun spice mix
- one tablespoon of black pepper
- one teaspoon of cayenne pepper
- one tablespoon of garlic powder
- one teaspoon of celery salt.
- Soak the wood chips in water for 1 hour.
- preheat the smoker to 200 degrees F.

Directions:

1. Trim off any fat, sinews, and silver skin, and rinse off any remaining hairs and dirt
2. Cut the venison about 1/4 inch thick
3. Blend ingredients making sure that the sugar is dissolved. You may have to warm the water.
4. Mix half of the marinade to the solution and gently stir until the marinade is absorbed.
5. Then add the rest of the marinade stirring slowly.
6. Let the jerky soak for at least an hour in the marinade.
7. Keep the smoker temperature between 180 to 200 degrees Fahrenheit.
8. Place the jerky on the grill in the smoker.
9. Check every hour until done.
10. Cooking time will take from four to six hours.
11. The jerky should be fairly dry, but still very pliable.
12. It will be about one-third its original size due to shrinkage.

Apple Duck Breast

Ingredients:

- 1 quart of apple juice or apple cider warm
- 1/4 cup kosher salt or 3 tbs canning salt
- 1 bay leaf crushed
- 1 clove of garlic crushed
- 1/2 tsp peppercorns cracked

Directions:

1. Soak the wood chips in water for 1 hour. Use apple or pear wood for the smoke.
2. Preheat the smoker to 225 degrees F.
3. Cut the bone and skin from the duck breast halves.
4. Blend the ingredients making sure the salt is completely dissolved in the solution.
5. Enough brine for up to 1 1/2 pounds of duck breast halves.
6. Soak the duck breasts in the brine for at least two hours or overnight is the best.
7. Give the duck a quick rinse and then pat dry with paper towels.
8. Brush each breast with melted bacon grease thoroughly.
9. Arrange the breasts on the grill in the smoker and start cooking.
10. Check the breasts every 35 minutes and flip over.
11. Duck is ideally eaten when medium rare. If you prefer well done take them out when the internal temperature reaches 170 degrees with a meat thermometer.

Wild Marinaded Goose

Ingredients:

- 2 cups brown sugar
- 1 cup black pepper
- 2 tsp garlic powder
- 2 tsp cayenne pepper
- 1 tsp red pepper flakes
- 1 tsp ginger
- 1/2 tsp soy sauce

Directions:

1. Soak the wood chips for 1 hour. Use your favorite wood to smoke
2. Preheat the smoker to 225 degrees F.
3. Mix the ingredients together in a small bowl. Set aside.
4. Rinse and clean up the breast halves.
5. Cut the goose breasts into 1/2 inch strips cutting them lengthwise.
6. Soak the goose breast in the marinade for eight hours.
7. Sprinkle a heavy coat of the seasoning mix.
8. Place on the grill in the smoker.
9. Smoke the goose at 200-225 Fahrenheit for 2 to 3 hours.
10. Check the breasts every 35 minutes and turn over.
11. Cook until the internal temperature is 170 degrees F with a meat thermometer.

Bacon wrapped Pheasant

Ingredients:

- pheasant breasts, skinned
- skin from leg quarters
- 2 whole
- 3 pieces cold water
- 1 quart Kosher salt
- 3 Tbs onion powder
- 1 Tsp garlic powder
- 1 Tsp dried parsley
- 1 Tsp dried parsley
- 1/2 Tsp white pepper
- 1/2 Tsp paprika

Directions:

1. Soak the wood chips in water for 1 hour. Use alder, cherry or apple wood for the smoker.
2. This will give the pheasant a light smoky flavor.
3. Preheat the smoker to 200 degrees F.
4. The pheasant is soaked in a weak salt brine overnight
5. Dissolve the salt in the cold water to make the brine.
6. Soak the pheasant in the brine overnight, but no more than eight hours.
7. Rinse the pheasant and dry them off with paper towels.
8. Mix up the spices in a small bowl fully.
9. Season the breasts lightly on all surfaces.
10. Wrap the bacon around the pheasant so it's covered completely.
11. When the bacon is in place, secure it with toothpicks.
12. Sprinkle a little more of the spice mix onto the skin.
13. Arrange the pheasant breast on the grill in the smoker.
14. Flip over every 30 minutes.

15. Smoke for four to six hours at 200 degrees Fahrenheit.
16. Cook until the temperature reaches 165 degrees F checking with a meat thermometer.

Bacon Dove

Ingredients:

- 12 dove breasts cut out the breast bone
- 1 bottle of Italian Salad dressing
- 1 tbsp Garlic Powder
- 1 tbsp Onion Powder
- 1 tbsp of Cajun seasoning
- 1 tbsp of freshly cracked pepper
- 20 jalapeño slices
- 20 tooth picks
- 7 slices of bacon cut into thirds

Directions:

1. Soak your favorite wood chips in water for 1 hour.
2. Preheat the smoker to 225 degrees F.
3. Mix all the ingredients in a small bowl. Set aside.
4. Soak the toothpicks in water for at least 30 minutes.
5. Trim all the fat off of the dove breasts.
6. Trim each dove breast off of the breast bone.
7. Stretch each piece of bacon and cut into 3 equal pieces.
8. Place a jalapeño slice next to each breast.
9. Wrap with bacon and push a toothpick through to lock in place.
10. Place each wrapped dove breast in the marinade.
11. Marinade for about 4 hours.
12. Take out of the marinade and place on the smoker.
13. Cook until bacon is done.
14. Check the dove breasts every 35 minutes.

Deer Ribs

Ingredients:

- salt and pepper
- garlic powder
- onion powder
- favorite herb and spice seasoning

Marinade Ingredients:

- honey
- apple juice
- brown sugar
- Blend equal amounts of the ingredients together and set aside.

Directions:

1. Soak your favorite wood chips in water for 1 hour.
2. Preheat the smoker to 225 degrees F.
3. Brush a heavy coat of the marinade on the ribs.
4. Put the deer ribs on the grill and start smoking.
5. Check the ribs and turn them over every 30 minutes.
6. Baste with marinade each time.
7. Cook until the ribs tear apart easily with a fork.
8. Cooking time is about 5-6 hours.

Conclusion

Char-Broil Grilling Cookbook for Beginners includes more than 100 tasty meat-focused recipes featuring innovative ways to add flavor and variety. There are even carnivore meal plans with grocery lists to make the diet easy to follow.

These clever recipes come from savvy home cooks who know how to pump up flavor with just a few ingredients, and now we're sharing those secrets in this brand-new collection.

Wait no more! Grab your copy now to enjoy you outdoor grilling and live better!

www.ingramcontent.com/pod-product-compliance
Lightning Source LLC
LaVergne TN
LVHW080300170625
813996LV00009B/244
9781915038661